AUDIO
ACCESS
INCLUDED

peed • Pitch • Balance • Loop

VIOLIN

CLASSIC POP SONGS

Audio arrangements by Peter Deneff

To access audio visit:
www.halleonard.com/mylibrary
Enter Code
2743-6517-8381-4329

ISBN 978-1-5400-0250-1

HAL•LEONARD®
7777 W. BLUEMOUND RD. P.O. BOX 13819 MILWAUKEE, WI 53213

Visit Hal Leonard Online at
www.halleonard.com

BRIDGE OVER TROUBLED WATER

VIOLIN

Words and Music by
PAUL SIMON

CANDLE IN THE WIND

VIOLIN

Words and Music by ELTON JOHN
and BERNIE TAUPIN

DUST IN THE WIND

VIOLIN

Words and Music by
KERRY LIVGREN

EVERY BREATH YOU TAKE

VIOLIN

Music and Lyrics by\nSTING

FIRE AND RAIN

VIOLIN

Words and Music by
JAMES TAYLOR

HAVE I TOLD YOU LATELY

VIOLIN

Words and Music by
VAN MORRISON

Slowly, with feeling

GOOD VIBRATIONS

VIOLIN

Words and Music by BRIAN WILSON
and MIKE LOVE

HEAVEN

VIOLIN

Words and Music by BRYAN ADAMS
and JIM VALLANCE

13

LEAN ON ME

VIOLIN

Words and Music by
BILL WITHERS

15

SHE'S ALWAYS A WOMAN

VIOLIN

Words and Music by
BILLY JOEL

WITH A LITTLE HELP FROM MY FRIENDS

VIOLIN

Words and Music by JOHN LENNON
and PAUL McCARTNEY

TEARS IN HEAVEN

Violin

Words and Music by ERIC CLAPTON
and WILL JENNINGS